That Time

ON THE

Mountain

Illustrations used with permission from Vecteezy.com and Freepik.com
Editing and book design by Jansina of Rivershore Books

ISBN: 978-1-63522-069-8

Printed in the United States of America
10   9   8   7   6   5   4   3   2   1

RIVERSHORE BOOKS

Rivershore Books
8982 Van Buren St. NE • Minneapolis, MN 55434
763-670-8677 • info@rivershorebooks.com

That Time on the Mountain

The mountain rose above and away from her,
This young maiden, so used to being alone.
She gardened and picked food from the forest
And asked for nothing but a shack for a home.

Halfway up the mountain, and directly above,
Lived the mountain man, silent, strong, alone.
He lived off the land from his deep dark cave.
He could face where the morning sun shown.

On a sun sparkled day, he went down to her shack.
They quietly met and then bathed in the stream.
She cut back his hair, and he served up a meal.
By first light he was gone, leaving, only a dream.

Time slid past 'til the forest bright-colored its plume
And the maiden caught her first bitter taste of alone.
She packed a small bag and let the rest stay.
She climbed to keep her heart from forming a stone.

They met and they flourished,
One to another, they nourished.

Together they watched the annual visit of a star.
It came with a glow that drew all cold away
And left warmth for them; both within and without.
It left with the rising sun, though they urged it to stay.

As is just the way of it, they loved and turned old,
And just for the fun of it, they dug for gold.

The star's time came due, and they watched the
Glow come into the cave, then open itself: extolling.
Together they shed their bodies to the cave floor.
Two souls flew, while dancing, into the star: enrolling.

They always knew but had never known,
The destiny they would now be shown.

Di Shibbe

A Dedication
For the encouragement

There's a lady living in our house,
Who makes all of it sparkle with life.
The one who has become its very center.
Now. Please, let me introduce my wife.

Though many times we've been shaken and tossed
Like dice in a cup.
When we really didn't know an escape, a direction,
Or which way was up.

We know, as couples too soon find,
That one or the other is doctor told
Of grave illness and uncertain future.
Through it all, both hands we hold.

And thanks, I must give, readily,
For sharing in the daily living,
That stretched for wondrous years

Of mutual taking and happy giving.

We've both enjoyed the times
Of which you've surely heard
Of days with doing nothing
And resting afterward.

So as gently as a wondrous melody
Caught in mind, repeated through and through,
With a cherished vow, I now repeat:
Phyllis: "I Love You."

Shimmering Moments

When you madly run atop crashing waves
Or look deep to the water's own reflection,
Dance on the shimmer of a babbling brook,
Adding to your days of dreams collection.

Grab the handle of the bright, full moon.
Pour out all its golden beams, begotten
And slide, slide, slide, and wildly slide
On rugged mountains, now soft as cotton.

In vivid imagination or heart-firmed faith,
You will never consider any as "odd"
To lean forward in quiet gladness,
Feeling the soft, warm breath of God.

The Remembering Man

He was an old timer, who brings up a memory
Faster than most or anyone can.
He knew what came after, then what came next.
They called him, in awe,
"The Remembering Man."

He lived on our block, just two doors down,
Gathering in folks from all over our town.

He sat out on the porch in long underwear.
You see, for a fashion, he just didn't care.
Folks who came by sat in attendance,
Concerned in the facts that he'd share.

They got to know what came before,
And, who did what and did it when.
If you were real quiet, respectful, and
He'd surmise how it really ought to have been.

More and more people heard of his doings.
They crowded, fussed, demanding a lot.
He revealed more than oddly known facts;
He began to distort, fictionalize the plot.

Soon one-third of the whole world heard of the man
And as news-folks and bloggers blogged out his fame,
He viewed his trashed lawn; folks and their leavings,
Then the "Remembering Man" forgot his own name.

Wind Chimes

Went to buy wind chimes,
Listened to them all.
Hearty gongs in deep tones,
Tiny stems ringing small.

Listened to wooden ones;
Thought it all a tease,
The sprinkling of a melody,
Announcements of a breeze.

Patiently, I picked and tried
The sounds they made, inside.
Selection more than I thought,
Found a set, those I bought.

There they hang, you see,
Centered on the deck, high above,
Catching each and every breeze,
Sounding off with softest love.

Frisky winds, started up,
Set the chimes to awful clanging.
Against the wind-driven frenzy;
Tied them up to stop the banging!

No longer are they cymbals,
But give up a whining toot.
The wind again gets even,
And plays them like a flute.

I lost the quiet tinkling, and
Did stop the wind-made clash.
I think I'll have to dump them.
Deep within the weekly trash.

Enough Was Enough?

Daryl Jasson had a sharp
And waking thought:
"Where's the birthday gift
He should have bought?"

Then he slid from
Her warm, warm bed.
"She asleep?" She
Hadn't moved her head.

Simple plan: Get some roses
Bright and red
And serve her breakfast, right
There in bed.

He took her car to be
Quiet and discreet,
And smoothly drove
On up the street.

A mile away, he saw café
Called the "Toast."
They did quick take-out,
Great coffee roast.

Crowded curbs-to park?
He'd find his own.
Slipped into a bus stop;
A tow-away zone.

Hair uncombed, shirt undone,
In morning nervous,
Stepped inside, wait his turn.
He asked for service.

"It will take a few," was the rule.
"Take a seat."
"Time needed"; left
On quick feet.

Against the light,
No time to beat,
To the flower shop,
Across the street.

Mission done, he could relax, better
Than he thought, by far.
Balanced food, flowers, and coffee,
Headed back to the car.

Another break, no ticket yet,
Good life was unblocked.
Tried the driver's door and
Found it tightly locked!

Looked in the glass, saw keys
Stuck in the ignition.
On the seat, his phone, with
No usable transmission.

Trudged back to the Toast
With hoarse and quiet moan,
"Please keep these warm;
"May I use your phone?"

Sleep slid quickly as she answered
On the second ring.
She listened as the tale unwound,
Said not a single thing.

Tired and upset, gave her
Car keys a quick nab.
Then hit the corner curb;
Deftly hailed a cab.

There at the bus-stop towing zone
Her car sat, still un-marked.
She slid in, started it, moved a gear,
And immediately embarked.

All should know her hurt and anger,
For clarity and for feel.
His phone she had placed, just ahead
Of the left rear wheel!

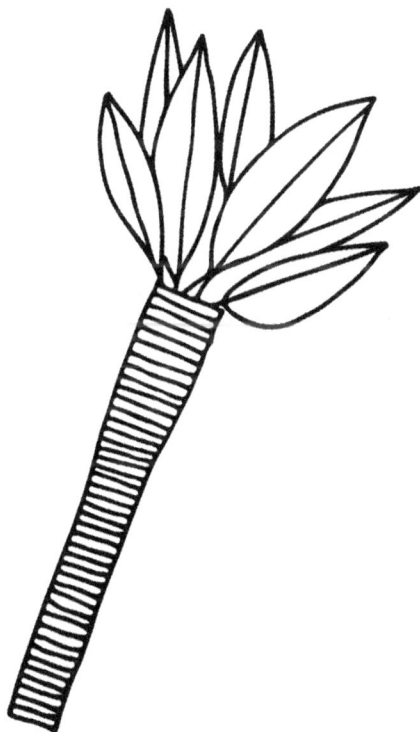

Seasonal Selling

I'll not try to sell you anything;
No, indeed, I sure will not!
I've just found a wondrous thing,
That I know you haven't got.

It's for that time you're finally done,
Spent hours lighting up the place.
Set the tree and outdoor lights,
Maybe it's time to light your face!

It's called: *Thompson's Teeth Tinsel*
To give everyone a happy bequeath.
'Cause when it's worn near a lamp,
You light up like a sparkling wreath.

It attaches to your upper teeth
And widely amplifies your grin,
Holds secure in kisses and food,
And hangs just under your chin.

There are those who, slightly blinded,
Will mutter a sneer: "Glitter Mouth!"
That simply means you did well
And they suffer from "happy drouth!"

Let them grouse, groan, and grumble.
You do know that you've done well.
And I really hope you make a buy;
I've got ten one-runner sleds to sell!

Right? Right!

What have you got to be
Embarrassed about?
What made your face turn red?
What does happen to jar
Your comfort or make you
Wish you were gone or dead?
You can't let them get you down.
Don't let anyone boss you around!
Keep in mind, one true fact,
That no matter how you act,
Then you will finally learn:
What they think of you
Is none of your concern!

A Significant Matter

It is likely, I somewhat hazily noted,
That the man for whom I had voted
Was, they said, "Mad as a Hatter."
That, I insist, is a significant matter.

When for parents whose teens,
In those ripped and torn jeans,
On each other do commit assault and much batter,
Parents can insist, it is a somewhat significant matter.

Or for those who shop until they are just bushed,
And from those behind who are rudely pushed.
But mostly from clerks who would rather chatter
Than offer service. Agreed, it is a significant matter.

And, too, the lovers who caught in their fight,
Neither can figure who's wrong or who's right,
Until one of them says their bond he will shatter.
To her then, we know, it is a significant matter.

Then will the drivers driving wild in the night,
And never preview a move to the left or right,
You guess for the left, they choose the latter.
You can insist, it's a most significant matter.

Consider the heftier woman who must diet,
Can barely ward off signs that say: "Buy It!"
No matter how little she eats, keeps getting fatter.
"You know," she cries out, "It's a significant matter!"

The best though is those two old, tottering geezers,
Who have short breath and suffer the wheezers.
They will argue through sputter and spatter,
We seriously doubt it is a significant matter.

The Lunch-Brunch Meeting

Here's a situation you may
Or may not have considered;
It seems unlikely that this
Sets your heart all a-twittered.

Nonetheless, and I'm guessing,
It is simply a thought, a hunch,
That you will find this of interest,
In this planned lunch, or brunch.

It happened quite casually
Just a gathering of old cronies.
To meet late Sunday morning,
For teas and jabbing balonies.

So, between them all, calls
And confirms were made.
Directions and cautions,
With bright plans were laid.

First to arrive were civilly greeted,
But cautioned: "All must arrive,
Before you can plan to be seated!"

They in good nature milled
To greet each friend on arrival.
As time went by, hunger grew,
That asked chance of survival?

In nearly a lifetime, they've gone quiet.
The last couple came, fresh with chatter.
Then all of them trooped up to the host
Who intoned: "Something's the matter!"

Standing as tall as his frame would allow
"I'm most glad you came, but I must say:
Your reservation was day before yesterday!"

At this they grumped and recoated,
Then hit the sidewalk, tight, a thicket.
Passerby edged around their huddle
And heard: "This just ain't cricket!"

They sputtered and then all agreed
To head for a place not quite so nice,
A noisier, brighter, plasticed palace
With coffee at a discounted price.

There's no moral to happy endings,
Attempt a review or backward glance.
Just this an oddly done gathering,
Be noted, "a happy happenstance."

Guardian Angel

I'm your guardian angel,
I move twice as a wink.
That's about twice as fast
As you can safely think.

To keep up with you,
Is really tough to do.

It would be much better
For you to take a break.
It's just the point
I'm trying to make.

Think of this when
It all gets tough,
Live in today,
Let that be enough.

Searching

Sometimes you must sift
Through most all the day,
Call forth its golden center.
A nugget which gives the day
Its meaning and its glow.
Not just clinging at the edges
But grabbing the full of life's
Sails and letting them fill,
Sweeping you through to
All your dreams and wishes.

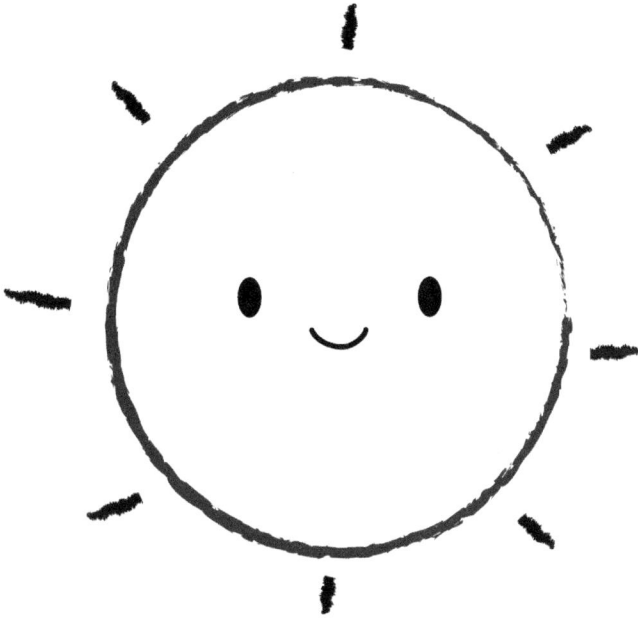

Sunning

Languid as a cat,
Lazy and baking
In the summer sun.
Warm breezes move
Over all my parts.
Warming, soothing,
Body areas seldom
Warmed, exposed
Tender spots;
Enjoying the sleep
In calm, steady heat.

Summer Day Dreams

I stepped over sunbeams
Displayed cross the sky;
Angled through storm clouds
about a half mile high.
I am alone with playful winds,
Churning clouds as cotton gins.

Watching thunder chatter the snare
Pounding frantic rhythms on a kettle,
Inviting lightning to spark and flare,
Allowed to spear ground-based metal.

Half a mile up and close to me,
seen through the old oak tree
Minds bring scenes so close they seem
Illustrated better through a dream.

Just Being Dumb

Nothing is more fun than dumb.
It should be practiced every day.
So, try do a thing, really stupid!
It helps to blow them all away.

Everyone can do a very crazy thing,
Without being too panicking chaotic.
It comes easier as you go forth and
It will seem you've turned, psychotic.

Maybe consider that being dumb,
Means to show you cannot speak.
As they lean close to hear your words,
It's time to release a horrid screech!

When you raise more eyebrows,
That cause a face furrowing frown,
Now as they point and laugh.
You've gained the rank of clown.

Lost in a Corn Maze

On a quiet Saturday,
I took a quiet drive.
Never thought when I began
I might not get home, alive.

Doddering down a country road
I spied a bright lit pumpkin farm,
Next to a sprawling corn field
To stop, it seemed no harm.

These fine offerings they had
Held my thoughts and my gaze.
Soon I spotted the challenge
To trod the corn-field maze.

But first, a truly quenching drink,
A spot of icy apple cider.
Several glasses did I down.
You smile grew wider.

Thus fortified with vim and sugar,
I paid the toll to enter in the maze
And found the path wide and easy.
I moved within a sun-baked daze.

So confident, I took each tum
'Til I found a spot without a bend.
Then spun around just to find
I'd truly entered a real dead end.

Now that's just silly, simply nuts;
My mind refused to pay the cost!
On something not even rational,
And to believe I'm truly, truly lost!

I scuttle back along the path,
Sure that the exit would be near.
Took several turns in my rush and
Found I had advanced to the rear!

Panicked now and wild with worry,
"I am here!" that's what I did shout.
The sound collided with a laugh,
"Yes, you are!" from some calloused lout.

The thoughts still nagged and persisted.
"Would I wander corn-caught 'til I die?"
Stood on tip-toe to get a clearer view,
"How come this crop is ten foot high?"

Night has come and stars pop out.
"That the North Star? The big dipper?"
Don't know why I even bothered,
I can't tell them from the Lady Slipper.

"Enough and Enough!" my mind cries.
"I can breach these small, spindly stalks
I'll just smash right through and be free,
Then swear off forever these eerie walks!"

I gather up my last strength and crash,
I've hit my head, a hurtful, fearsome crack.
With swirling stars warping up my mind,
I see I've smacked against the cider shack.

In stumbling movements to the parking lot
I find the car and blessed I am, it awaits.
Thanking the muffler's soft and quiet purr,
Drive the vehicle out those enticing gates.

OH, YES!
You remember the quantities of cold cider
That sugared up to be the path's decider?
I found a corn-stalk corner to be hid
And couldn't, shouldn't, but yes, I did!

To this day, on no return am I tempted;
I've not called, nor asked to be redempted.

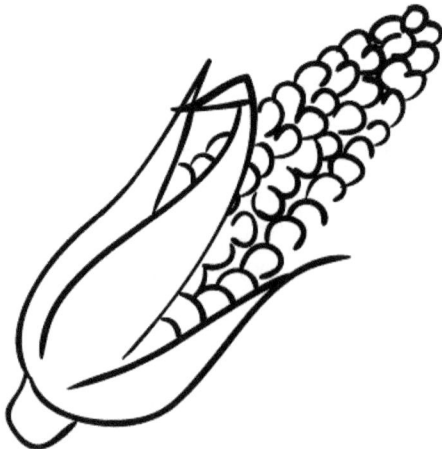

Deadline

I'll take my time,
I say at last.
I'll use more time,
Review the past.
Maybe waste a day or two
Find a park to wander through.
Spend a day, or just a night.
That's true? That's my right!
I'll simply use them all,
Minutes and long hours,
'Til they're really gone
Like long-dead flowers.
Then when the final
Deadline appears,
I'll work double hard
Despite my fears!

Shake out the folds

Of the flannel
In your mind.
Make a cozy
Tent to these,
To sit beneath
Warm, quiet
And enjoy
The grace of
Winter.

Past

How long should history last?
When can we forget the past?

Hurts caused the heart to fester
Can become the mind's molester.

It is time to see far ahead,
Let our memories play dead.

It is time to forget and forgive,
To find a mindful way to live.

Stand Tall, Veterans!

You signed up.
You Volunteered!
For that alone,
You should be cheered!

Look in your mirror,
And say out loud:
"I'm a veteran;
I stand proud."

The Darkest Time

I suspect there is a lesson in value
To be discovered and maybe learned.
Be digested, notated, locked in memory.
For societies' sake, not simply spurned.

Through most of his near adult life,
Tracy Stidman worked as a petty thief;

Picked up a little of this, a little of that,
Carefully avoiding self-inflicted grief.

In light of day and with full-faced smiles,
I'm sure you've seen him, know the type:
Completely calculating, and easily stealing
Apples, thirty seconds before they're ripe.

Qualified, he has become, he lives well.
Tracy keeps his business quite small.
He's had many close brushes with the law.
He knows the results of a harsh judge's call.

Now on this nice and profitable night,
Tracy Stidman finds a truth many share:
"It's always darkest just before spotlights
Bloom and wailing sirens truly scare."

Without recourse, the judge sentenced a term,
And asked, "When done, where will you go?"
Tracy Stidman answered, straight as he could:
"Back to my old job, it is about all I know."

There is no Wrong Turn Lane

Consider if you will, or might,
A reason to complain:
There's lanes for left and right turns,
But there is no wrong turn lane.

Then add this cautious thought,
Turn by mistake, read: "incorrect."
And the next road you select,
You obviously won't connect!

The highway folks offer no solution,
We do hope they will somehow relent,
Or add a lane for those who didn't know,
Save them from a car-crushing event.

Summing it all up, with a stern nod to the law:
To read a book, or dial your phone,
Or take a turn with no look nor signal,
That's a wrong turn; you're on your own!

And just in case you would digress,
Two wrongs make you socially diminished,
But skillfully done, and carefully too,
Take three rights; your left turn is finished.

Goes Down The Drain

Please imagine, if you will,
An actor chases after fame.
With one forgotten speech,
His career is down the drain.

Still, it may be much harder
With attempts to explain,
How you try and really try,
And all goes down the drain.

Thoughtfully, there is a plus,
And it pertains to the rain.
It would be simply awful if
It didn't go down the drain.

OK, that's the most of it.
Only adding a quick refrain,
You must hold on, oh so tight,
Before it all goes down the drain.

Hello Again!

When did I see you?
How Long ago?
What was the weather?
Did it snow?

Hours and days
Do flow past.
We know sunshine
Does not last.

We both have stories
We have to tell.
With jokes, and lies,
In a comic spell.

Did you visit royalty
In a foreign land?
Or have you dreamed
something really grand?

These are stories
I'd love to hear,
So please come
And sit right here.

Until You Hear a Baby Cry

You watch the clutter of moving folks
Bent, wandering, they've only a sigh;
Again we try to ignore their plight
Until, at last is heard, a baby's cry!

Give me your tired, your poor, your huddled masses
Yearning to breathe free;

The boats are full to mocking death
Shuddering under a stove hot sky
We look away from crashing waves
Until we finally hear all babies' cry.

The wretched refuse of your teeming shore,

Starving masses stumble through
Baked, crusted earth burned dry.
With weak belief there's water near.
Can we not hear lost people cry?

Send these, the homeless, tempest tossed to me.

Maybe, we can't feed the world, each one,
And give them all a safe, dry place to lie.
Will we still feel we've not the means,
As we finally hear the last baby's cry?

I lift my lamp beside the golden door!

My thanks to the Lady in the Harbor, also known as
the Statue of Liberty.

Buy Now

Things I wish I could buy,
Go to the store and try:
Things like an extended arm
To reach without doing harm.
A onehanded way to pitch a tent.
A skunk that comes without a scent.
A car that knows where I want to travel.
And on the ice, spreads out gravel.
And finally, I really need to buy,
A guide who knows: "why!"

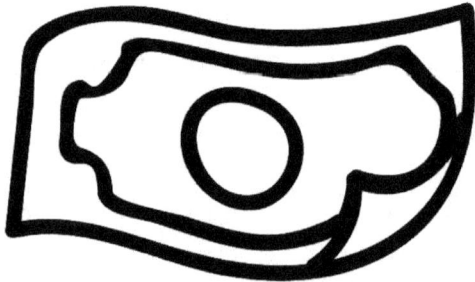

Two

Two smiles aimed at each other
In the near dark.
One tear sliding down a cheek,
Two smiles aimed at each other,
In the near dark.

Two hands holding two hands,
One tear sliding down a cheek,
Two smiles aimed at each other
In the near dark.

Says everything.

Attention

We suppose what is needed
With honorable mention,
Is the wide-ranging usage
That called for "attention."

First is "paying attention,"
And say, "What the heck."
If they supply an address,
We'll send them a check.

Then we hear, "attention please,"
Which we deem awfully polite.
We perk up, look up, smile,
Hope the "word" comes out right.

An opposite side of this cause,
That causes much hypertension,
Are the military's harsh orders:
"Army! One. Be at attention!"

Others do study our attention span,
Stretched through hours of chatter,
In our inability to bridge a silly thought
With the conclusion: "It doesn't matter."

Finally, a firmly required challenge,
Without a tiny speck of dissention,
We must fight with vigor and honor,
For the quiet of attention retention.

Teasing Note

On the walking path
Around our urban lake,
There was a painted note.
It caused a double take.

There in flowing script,
Sprayed white on gray,
Seen, as I approached a
Lover's secret on display.

We all know that writing on
Public property is so wrong,
Be it a love letter, or even
The words of a private song.

Was then I finally realized
And felt a mild disgrace.
There so neatly written,
"Remove and Replace."

I Am The Honkinater

When traffic is way too slow,
Folks just can't seem to go,
I give them all a great blow!

If they edge in my lane,
I'll call out a bad name
Then honk out my fame.

I've slipped through a red light
And answered all honks with spite.
They should know it's my right!

I'm the driving relater,
Often hot as
boiled tater,
Cause I'm the Honkinater!

Last Country Dance

He helped her from the folding chair.
Watched her tuck away a lock of hair.
She whispered, "Remember, you lead."
"Go easy, we're not a tumbleweed!"
"One two three, one two three."
The Band opened with a soft fiddle
And caught the rhythm by guitar.
The couple slowly moved to the edge
The youngsters centered the floor.
"One two three, one two three."
They trade smiles, holding tight.
She worried her skirt, once white.
He hummed a tune of their first night.
They asked the band, "One more verse?"
She smiled, and nodded; he grinned.
"One two three, one two three."
His legs got tired as if he'd sinned,
And she sagged against his chest.
"One two three;" "One two three."
Brought them back to their table.
Trading smiles, "We are a fable."

To My Valentine

I love you
You love me
Just what else
Could there be?

We do hold hands
And sing and dance,
And laugh so hard
We wet our pants.

Then eat ice cream
With goo and such
But that might be
A tad too much.

So, let's just wait
And we will see,
Just what else
This could be.

Advice on Marriage

He stood before them
With furrowed brow,
Ready to explain
The "do's" and "how."
He had great advice
That needed shared.
They knew, he knew,
They knew he cared.
His hands wandered
Lost, then fluttered,
Landing in deep pockets.
No words he muttered.
Again he about faced,
Then turned back around,
And with a large harrumph,
Stuck out his chin
Like Andy Gump.
As finally he spoke,
His voice came out flat.
"Just", he paused, "Let
Me get back to you on that."

All Over

The late-setting moon
Puts a pattern in the sky.
And maybe that's why
Your kite won't fly.
Or why the earliest
Birds can't cry.
With a most heavy sigh,
The long days of summer
Just said goodbye.

My Mental Marathon

Stood by the side,
Watched them run.
Now, I told myself,
That would be fun!

Checked the schedule
And did pick one.
Stood with the crowd
Awaiting the gun.

I'd trained for
A solid three days,
Fully knowing that
Preparation pays!
Now we start and
So does pain!
Both legs are hurt,
I'm going insane!
Stumbled into a
Runner's behind.
Fell on someone
She was unkind!
EMTs came running,
And I think I'm dead.
This run's in my head.

Winter's Here

Soft welcome snowflakes
Cover dark autumn brown.
Not revealing their intent:
For harsh cold mornings:
With too quiet nights.
Nothing dares move
Against the silence.
In ear snapping cold,
Your footsteps complain
On hard crusted snow.
You fear being followed,
Closely.

A Pun is Fun

Don't stare and click your teeth
And to me sour looks bequeath.
I reached far beyond the sun
To drop a clinker of a pun.

There is a town in Minnesota
By the grand old name of Hines.
Do listen before your whines!
Know this before we really fight,
This town's home of "Hines-Sight."

Sharing a Zippo Lighter

I'd like to make a great suggestion,
And on this you can certainly depend.
There is nothing in this whole world,
Like sharing a Zippo with a friend.

The one we had was bent and scarred,
Was neither bought nor stolen.
We found it back of the Five and Dime:
Owned by angry, Mr. Henry Scollen.

The Zippo wouldn't light at first,
And we learned its rule of fire:
It needed flint and a can of fluid,
Plus a thumb that wouldn't tire.

Don't overfill or it will leak,
From pocket onto leg, a fireless burn.
Or it might engulf itself in a fiery ball
When the wheel hits its second turn.

To snap and light it with one hand,
And in that motion send it higher.
My friend would catch it, flip it back:
Still lit, in a wild, hot arc of fire!

To have a Zippo and a friend
Was just perfectly swell.
But then if I remember,
It had an awful smell!

For All Those Years

For All Those Years,
No matter how it's said.
We linger for a moment,
The thought goes dead.

True with astonishment,
A fuzzy picture, faint.
Married all these years,
One must be a saint.

Know the smell of Spring,
That time in fifty-five,
We were young, restless,
So very much alive.

There were tough times,
To season, build, knowing,
Challenges kept us close,
All helped our growing.

Add wildly joyous times,
Laughter beyond caring,
Holding tight, making plans,
Showing well our daring.

Think of all our years,
As one, to applaud,
Guided by a gentle faith
The caring voice of God.

The Whistling Man

I came upon the whistling man
He, without effort, hit every key.
I bet he knew a thousand songs.
That's what it seemed to me.

Was he sharp or was he flat?
I'm not the one who can tell.
He knows the songs, complete
And, as I said, does them well.

The more I listened to his whistle,
I'll bet I knew them all, every word.
His whistling captured all the notes,
Better than any I've ever heard.

At last my listening had to lapse,
As a certain song struck a memory.
It was then I finally and fully knew,
The whistling man was really me.

Well, I Gotta Go Now

You wonder where they'd
Rather be,
Or maybe where you would
Rather be?

When you make a comment
About a friend, that's not true
And you hear a soft "oh"
'Cause she's just behind you!

When you walk into the room,
The talk goes quickly quiet.
You hear in the echo of talk:
"She should be on that diet!"

When you sped through that light
Now not yellow, but slightly red,
Colored lights, with siren start,
You should have stopped, instead.

When the judge states the fine cost
And his gavel makes the final drop,
You know the checkbook's empty
So clear: you should have stopped!

When the boss is out of earshot
You whisper, "He's a stupid ass!"
He didn't leave the room at all;
You just got a lifetime pass.

The Worm Farm Owner

In the wonderful world of
Make believe,
I've got something that might
Tug your sleeve.

Out back on our lawn,
Seen, just after dawn,
A strutting robin,
Filled with alarm.
Patrolling the edges
Of his own worm farm.

His head bobs, as he wonders,
Tilts as he thinks, "blunders"
How he might intercede
In case of stampede.

Never mind that he hired
Two robins as worm-pokes,
And had to put up with
Their very sick jokes.

After their eating,
Left him bereft.
When they were full
They just up and left.

Now he must consider
Do or die, leave a widder?

Nope, he thinks.
Here are the facts,
Herding earthworms is
harder than cats.

Alone, he struts the perimeter,
realizing without alarm
Nothing, not by one centimeter,
Will harm or help this worm-farm.

With that, he flies up. Goes on his way.
He'll check back. Maybe next Friday.

Called a Sin

This list is long, so very layered,
I scarcely know where to begin.
This counting of transgressions;
They all nod: "Now that's a sin!"

Even from a young and tender age
Where basic knowledge is so scant,
We are warned against several thoughts
That boil parents and pastors up to rant.

So what's a kid supposed to know?
Can he see what has never been?
If even a casual carnal observance
Is quickly cast as a mighty sin?

Add to the mess, a qualifying degree of lapse
To be rated beyond the most hard-in-all.
What affront breaks the most righteous rules
To bring a sin up to the rank of cardinal?

If you wish to crest the mountain top and
Then, perhaps, permit the greatest chortle,
As you taste the flavor of beyond belief:
"That sin, yea that sin, is classed as mortal!"

There is a method to modify your degradation,
At the point you are not able to fail or function.
All you've done, or thought, or said, or dreamed,
Is all gone as you receive an oily dose of Unction.

To recapitulate, sum up, and reach a fine solution,
To this business of sin that is somewhat overblown,
There is no answer, no retort, or satisfying reply,
For folks who remind: "You should have known!"

About Your Accident

We think, it's so strange,
As life begs silently to interrupt,
Holds the walker to an accident;
Without preview, so abrupt!

But those skids did predict the fall
Ending in a groan packed whoosh.
Adds quick pain and embarrassment,
"You could still be on your tush!"

"No use," I say, "No use at all!"
You can't point your pointer finger
And cry, "You pushed me!" That's
Sadly, hurting, bound to linger.

As a somewhat carefree proclamation:
"I think I've said all I can wisely tell
With a sense of languid, lazy urgency,
Do have calming rest until you're well."

The Sentencing

To you, old wet Jacket:

You shall hang on a metal hanger

On the nearest clothesline,

That you can be viewed

By all others,

Wearing similar outer garments!

You will hang until your fabric

Reveals, without question, that you

Have gone straight and are dry and

Fit to be worn in public again!

A Gotta List

I've got a list
Of what I gotta do.
It's very, very long
Now I'm telling you.

I gotta sit right down,
And write a long letter;
I've gotta make a banker
Feel so much better.

I gotta take a short break
To catch up on my reading.
Then I gotta till the garden,
To finally start the seeding.

I gotta get to the store
To stock up on some vittles.
Then put some fertilizer
Where puppy always piddles.

For a list of really gottas,
I'll say that it's a wrap.
The time for lists is over.
I've got to take a nap.

The County Park

Take a walk with me, I do implore;
Through our county park we'll explore.
Blacktopped path, built for skaters,
Runners and bikes.
And for Mom and Me, three mile
Really long hikes.

"Bike on left!" heard from the rear;
"Left?" stepped left, bike so very near.
The rider braked and locked his knees,
I hear him crash through the trees.

Dog off leash, left his droppings,
Runs at us, barking, stopping!
I just stood there, petrified,
And what I said is classified.

Soaring eagles, egrets, mud ducks,
Squirrels, a fox, but not a deer.
We're too noisy to let them come
Anywhere close to see or hear.

Now, look it here, almost done,
Back to where we parked the car.
Made the circle through the park,
Can't believe we walked that far.

A Cure For Mental Mold

I went deep in the doldrums
And on to self-defeating gloom.
I walked in a sullen, surly funk
That did seem to cloud the room.
It's obvious that the only cure:
Sunshine and sugared food,
Well mixed with ribald laughter
Forcing me into a better mood.

I searched all the hidden places
Looked for chocolate or candy,
It seemed just too much work,
Nothing edible, near, or handy.

Still hurting and despondent,
I came upon some chocolate icing,
And found some new made lefse;
They looked to have a magic zing.

To add a taste to the gift of lefse,
We've known the oddest pairing,
Spread evenly and rolled tight,
Like mustard with pickled herring!

Tried the chocolate, thickly.
Then I saw a truer goal,
Double up the freshest lefse
Around a large Tootsie Roll!

You'll never know
'Til you try it.
I've never thought
To ever hide it.

Waltzing With The Angels

Waltzing with the angels,
It's easy as can be
All you need to know is
How to count to three.

And the special rule:
You don't have to lead.
Nor to watch your feet.
Shoes you don't need.

Up and round the clouds
To sparkling stars, you'll fly.
You'll hear notes of music
As it swirls the midnight sky.

Up to the milky way,
Then Mars' rings,
Pine tree limbs,
Stalks of corn
Upon river's rapids
And clear, flat lakes.

Waltzing with the angels
It's easy as can be.
All you need to know is
How to count to three.

To Quiet An Echo

You can't quiet an echo by shouting,
And it's no help to use your pouting.

Listen now! I'll say it straight:
Anger roils and tempers shudder
The whole crowd yells and swears,
Some so mad, they simply sputter.

Spit rolls down as faces bloom,
Hands shake, teeth tightly clench,
That's the time to grab the pail.
Be sure that everyone is drenched.

Now see the grander folly,
Drying slowly cools tempers.
Before you get back to pouting,
Echoes never quiet by shouting.

Witch Hazel

As I lay sleeping, so hard and deep,

Who pulls the covers off my feet?

Who makes the babies coo and laugh?

Who wakes them up, after a bath?

Who opens the door to walk my floor?

Who climbs my stairs when no one's there?

Who twirls my hair into a terrible mess?

Who dumps my clothes upon the floor?

Who dirties my carpet so my peer can see?

Who whispers nonsense into my head?

Who blows so soft it tickles my ear?

Who moves the things that I hold dear?

Who moves with me wherever I stray?

Who causes the hounds at night to bay?

Who is this creature now at hand?

Who can forget a name so grand?

Whose name is known to all our kin?

Who makes us wish what might have been?

Course, that's Witch Hazel!

By Steve Stokke ...April, 1995

Cause Yourself a Blister

"Mister!"

"You get in here and just sit down!"
He balanced a smile with a frown.
The old man winced from his pain,
Then eased on down with his cane.

"It's about your time?" he began.
"To go do a thing, get off your can?
Don't you think, really now, Mister,
You get a job? Cause a blister?"

"Frankly, you seem deep in doubt,
What you can do, or be without.
To ease your thoughts, I'll say this Mister:
"Just hit the road! Go cause a blister!"

"It's not so tough when you pay your way.
Please come visit, your first payday.
Grab your hat, board the magic twister.
Take pride in your first earned blister."

"Out in the world is a wonderful show,
There's no telling how far you can go!
But if you stay!
Please don't think that I'm not the kind.
I can still put that blister on your behind."

Waltzing with Wood ticks

Their favorite night was Saturday
To dance in the big, cleaned barn,
Waltzing with the Wood Ticks,
Where no one gave a darn.
All who gathered were in high spirits;
Laughing, meeting, drinking too.
They whirled but had to stop:
Someone yelled, "I lost a shoe!"
That was the signal, to be sure.
The band quickly changed the beat
They all knew which song came next,
To old time waltz with stomping feet.

And they all sang out:
"Itch – itch – itch"
"Scratch – scratch – scratch"
"Get it off! Get it off!"

Exhausted, they sat down,
Passed lots of high test draft
They rested, laughed, and
Sure, they swallowed
Enough to make them daft.
The band slowed the tempo to help
Them move together, so serene.
To dance the band's final set,
While they sang: "Good night Irene."

Simply Said

It is right that here and now
I need solemnly announce:
"When it comes to English,
I do not mispronounce!"

Seriously, I do remember
Ever since the second grade,
I learned to "sound it out."
After that, I had it made.

If you will write in simple fashion,
With no foreign language interaction,
I will enunciate all words perfectly;
Within a measured syllabletic fraction.

Honesty does require, I must reveal,
If you pretence and write in Freudian,
By rote, I will capsulate each line,
Speak in stammering awkwardian.

The Pallid Man

The weather finally warms,
We suffer thunderstorms.

But it's time to be alive and alert,
In walking shorts and short sleeve shirt!

Now walking with a bit of color,
Edged in flat off-white.
Does then force some observers
To comment on the site.

"Look at that man,
He's short and tan!
Should be called,
The 'Pallid Man!'"

Dreaming

Weeds and summer thunder,
Hot winds and big wood ticks,
When you dream of summer
These are Mom nature's picks.

Sunburn and no-seeums,
Belly flops in cold lakes,
When dreaming of summer,
This is really all it takes.

Baseball strikes and fish hook
Taken, hurting, through the ear,
When you dream of summer,
It's best you have a lot of beer.

Stinging wasps and loud cycles,
With outboards that don't start,
When you do dream of summer,
Are we all just not that smart?

And think now how to get there,
In freezing rain and sullen woe,
You can start by softly singing,
"Let it snow, let it snow, let it snow!"

Nothing for Anger

I've got nothing
To be angry about.
Nothing to make me
Stomp and shout.

I've looked to the sky,
Still high and dry,
Where birds still fly

The grass still green
Rocks are still rough.
We needn't get angry
To show we are tough.

Yep, I'll look around some more
And maybe find what's in store.
Then I duck down, bow my neck
Quietly say, "Aw, what the heck!"

Now I see to the evening west
Sunset's turned red laced fire,
Now flowing with streams of
Soothing thoughts that inspire.

I've really nothing
To get angry about.
Nothing to make me
Stomp and shout.

Out in Our Alley

As boys, we loved to play in our alley
Close to the house of mean old Sally.

She'd shout at us over her lopsided chin
We'd do our best to stand still and grin.

"I know all you boys so very well!
If you don't behave you will go to hell!"

She'd wildly wave her long walking stick
That could kill us all in one slashing flick.

With not ever a choice for fight or flight,
We knew she was birthed deep in the night.

While spewing wild curses she did advance,
We knew right then we had no chance.

Retreat we did and screamed out our fear,
And saved our laughs 'til she couldn't hear.

Now sure we'll play again in the alley,
Close to the house of mean old Sally.

Enter Stage Left

I slyly peek through the corner curtain,
one hundred folks who've come to stare.
Yes! I've rehearsed near to exhaustion,
But, dear God, must I stand out there?

And there, in the second row, center
Sits Mrs. Kathy, our uptight English teacher.
She's proofing tonight's playbill.
Why, dear God, did you birth that creature?

Farther back, sits Cousin Caroline and
Next are Aunty Janet and dear old Uncle Jed.
They expect me to make them truly proud.
But, dear God, I may as well be left for dead.

The whole audience is filled with neighbors
Who will hear me speak in a voice that quakes.
They will watch with laughs and elbow jabs.
Dear God, my knees announce the shakes.

The curtain rises far too quickly; I step out,
And hushed they become. I take the blame.
They expect a quick-paced burst of dialog.
Dear God, I can't even remember my name.

Words do come forth, much to my surprise.
They are full and crisp with matching action.
Then we're in the scenes of the second act,
I am wild with pride and self-satisfaction.

At last and at last, I speak my final lines,
The curtain drops and listen! Oh my God!
And "Oh My God!" I never even dreamed,
That when I bowed, they would applaud.

The Great Bovine Revolt

There are seasons for all of us.
Many tales, need twice be told.
So, I'm gonna tell a long one,
If I might be ever so very bold.

I intended to create an epic
In it a proud and grand story
Of honor, ploy and skullduggery
And rate it somewhat shy of gory.

So begin, I will and name
A tiny west Texas town,
The hidden village of Schwep,
Not worth the rank of noun.

Schwep had on its abutting acres,
Several herds of assorted cattle.
Cows that sulked and lay about,
Scarcely the type to cause a rattle.

But they chewed cud and talked crud.
They griped, "No matter what is said,
All of you just want us dead!"

The talk went on, and a plan was hatched.
From herd to herd, the plot was patched.
To march on with bovine flair
To meet en masse at the village square.

So on bellies, with little regard for limb or udder
They scuttled in awkward moves, no cries to utter.

No one saw them move as they crept into place.
No on in town knew their cows to place a face.
Soon, the old bulls gave a loud and frightful snort.
Scaring the young heifers, almost to a mort.

On they came, smashing through barns and sheds
Leveling most in their path, including flower beds!

Not much damage was done,
To be fair.
Soon they eclipsed the village
Square.

Then panting, stamping, balling
With tails high, they left their
Really wet 'n rancid calling!

The folks held a frantic meeting.
To change the sign held greeting:
"Welcome to Schwep . . .
Please be careful
Where you Step."

Sisters:
The Daily Call

Hi!

Hi back!

How you doing?

Oh, better.

Better?

Jeff hit me again.

Oh no, again?

This time, he had his gun in
His hand.

You OK?

Ear hurts. Get dizzy easy.

Did you see Doctor?

He says I should be careful
When I walk. And take my
Pills.

Pills?

I don't take pills. Jeff
Said we can't afford them.

And Jeff?

He was holding his finger in
Trigger guard. That hurt him.

Oh, my God, what next?

Junior has a gun.

Oh No!

Shot a guy, says he killed him.
Says gun went off too easy.

Did he get caught?

Nah, they gave him a new gun.

Where's the one he used?

They put it in the river.
It's in a place nobody would
Ever look.

Good God! You got plenty
Of hurt.

I'm doing OK, how you doin'?

Kids and work keep me
Pretty busy.

Well he left.

He says that three kids were
Not what he signed up for.

Don't know.
Said he needed
A different space.

Ya. Look, gotta get to work.
The bus is here. Call ya?

Yep, see ya. Love ya.

What about Gary?

He left?

Where'd he go?

That's rotten!

OK, call tomorrow?

You too.

Feet Understanding

Think about the size of feet.
We're all made most complete
When God added on our feet.

Then there came the challenge
For the wise,
The great debate, the choosing
Of the size.

Some are really longer than a foot
And some are smaller by more than half,
And shoe-makers note the differences,
And charge enough to make them laugh!

We big-footed fellows
Find it hard to cross the street
The cars go whizzing by
Nearly riding on our feet.

Good many folks like to cry
And more do like to whine,
Because shorter feet need go
Even farther to "toe the line."

And bigger feet do likely spread,
Step on things, make them dead.

Alas, we all have problems,
When going to and fro,
'Cause each has to chance:
"The stubbing of a toe."

There's really no rhyme nor reason,
I'm trying to be discreet.
No earthly reason that I can tell,
For so many sizes of people's feet.

Then I saw this lady,
With feet most large and wide,
If she in a cow-pie stepped,
There'd be no place to hide.

Praying to Our Son

Can you find your way
Home in the dark?

Maybe you're
Torn twixt terror
And temptation.

Charging around with
That warming smile,
Looking for someone
To engage and beguile?

We swear he signed one
Of the devil's own pact,
Our strange young man,
Where'd he learn to act?

How do we know
What let him astray?
Did we lead an example
And pave his way?

Likely true, likely right,
That we were who led.
Yet we're sure he knows
To be here, and in bed!

Not carousing about
Nor drifting alone.
Or simply standing idle,
Causing talk in the town.

But answer we know
Is our hope of redemption?
For raising a son ranks
'Tween terror and temptation

Patience, Patience, Patience

Patience should be instantly rewarded,
And then completely be recorded.
Isn't it enough to validate
The good we pledge to initiate?
That expectations for our cause
Be proof that we can really pause?

So logically and with chagrin,
Shouldn't patience pay for sin?
And why we call for patience,
When only noticed is its absence?

Then let this intent be solidly recorded:
Patience should be instantly rewarded!

Day's Ending

Night comes at its own pace,
With sunsets and growing shadows,
Lengthening the sun's departure.
An orchestra begins in the trees:
The serenade of the pines,
Cleansing the wind.
The moon plays with the night,
As early dark shows her brighter.
Splashing light on lakes and rivers,
Creating white wobbly patterns
Through trees and shrubs,
To catch the waves
Roiled by the wind.
The brightness moves,
Matching your speed,
Flashing on the water,
Calling in an ancient code.

From the USPO

The postal folks have it nailed,
Some things never to be mailed.
They talk of acids, bombs, guns, and such,
And other things that seem to matter much.

But for average folk, like you and me,
Mailing other stuff should never be.
I'll give example, if you'll hear:
Never send a Joan or John Dear.

And keep the really nasty and mad
Messages home 'til you're less sad.
Do keep the hot and lust-full letter;
Just save it 'til you know her better!

We should all think before we send;
The stir we cause might never end.

Cowboy's Lament

I washed out my socks
Lay back on my saddle
I've spent the whole day
Chasing after your cattle.

So get out of my mind,
And give me a break.
Or I'll take a sample
Of those walking steak.

I'll imagine a fire
Searing the meat,
Check for doneness,
And then take a seat.

But to see the rest
Of cow just lying,
Just going to rot,
I'd start crying.

I'll look at the stars,
Spot one so near.
Another imagine:
An icy cold beer.

My body's so sore,
The whole thing is aching.
Just need to sleep before
Tomorrow's sun baking.

I'm staying right here,
'Til my breath's last rattle.
I'm staying right here,
Chasing after your cattle.

A Poet's Lament

The Prof dropped the paper
On the desk.
He looked right at me
And addressed the rest:

"A poet you are not
If that's all you got!"

"If you dropped this on the floor,
It will simply shatter.
All the words this badly used,
Will run, hide, scatter!"

"Just do it all over.
And work for pure poetry.
Spend you some real time,
provide some owe-it-tree!"

And working hard
With painful fuss,
Burned midnight oil,
becoming Sisyphus.

By daybreak, had
It all down,
Laid on his desk,
A writer's crown.

One last glance,
A spelling error!
A perfect chance
To feel terror.

Now reason came,
Maybe odd insight,
He reads lots
Miss it, he might!

OK now listen and do
Please have your say,
There's a huge rock
Heading my way.

Genesis

A beacon of quiet insistence is
A soft nudge toward a goal:
A dimly lit idea,
That is known and believed,
If only on the surface of the mind,
Or caught on a corner of the soul.

Back when we were friends

We could have an awful spat
Yet be back in nothing flat
To map our path and drives.
Too soon.

Too many roads, too many faces
No time now to review the years,
'Til the quiet of age softly appears
And calls back forgotten places.

Remember when we were friends?
In our hearts, we've made amends
And could laugh in nothing flat.

Those times we let hours stand
Held in quiet, our inner fears
Yet unafraid to share our tears.
Then countless others entered
Catching our thoughts, desires,
Shared the moments and the fires.

Harmony

Harmony comes from different voices and different people,
Voicing different notes, from different throats, sounds disparate—
Traveling along, but locked together in a wondrous pathway;
Called as if the universe directs the union of those feeling separate.

Immerse yourself in the turbulent waters
Where you can breathe even inside a rock.
Taste the rhythms of the drumbeats,
Feel all the harmonics you can and cannot see.

Wish for nothing beyond the grace of knowing
Splendidly free thoughts, unfettered, open,
Ready to receive and rejoice in the knowing
You are intrinsically inside all harmonies.

There is an understanding of the harmonies,
There where language becomes everyone's alike,
There where the voiceless are voiced and centers sought,
There is where peace and alikeness are celebrated.

Go then and listen in awe to the harmonics,
In the music, in the talk, in the valleys of all the mountains,
On the barren land and once again into the now quiet waters
Blend your voice in the harmonics.
You can create peace.

A blossoming peace within you and spreading openly,
To quiet anger, to still argument,
to open channels of quiet conversation,
And laughing in the proven path to agreement.
Then you are breathing in a rock,
You have created peace.

Springtime in December

The weather guys and gals danced out their forecast,
Barely able to hold back: "A storm is coming, at last!"

Even the somber-faced guy, explained the whys and the how:
"We will see a good snowfall; enough to shovel and to plow."

"Tomorrow!" they warned: "Beware the morning drive."
"Be cautious, go slow, take your time, get there alive!"

The sand and the plow trucks were loaded and put ready.
Drivers were tested to be awake, and sober, and steady.

Hundreds of pickups got plows and snow blowers were started.
Shovels were found and placed near for use, if only half-hearted.

Snow lovers and snow-mobile owners prayed to the sky;
Pledging eternal nice-ness for drifts over twelve feet high.

The very next morning did hold a promise to
break the dull look of this mid-winter's warm:
Dark clouds, slashing winds, a blizzard type hint,
Looked like this decade's first really great storm!

By noon, sullen clouds camped right over our space,
Released thirty-eight snowflakes that all seemed to race
In odd swirling patterns, in fact they just churned,
Then landed abruptly; they all crashed and burned.

In arithmetic fact and speaking with tongue-tied thrift.
This snowfall was sixteen gazillion flakes short of a drift.

Pundits explained: "A winter snowfall is meant to be aesthetic."
And they recapped: "The result of this storm is rated: 'pathetic.'"

A caucus of Methuselah-aged friends found it hard to remember,
When they ever before had to suffer a Springtime in December.

A World Without – N

It's time to report – to send a release!
News that will shatter – your idea of peace.

A group of "Publicdems" have just met
To cause more reductions,
To lighten all loads,
Not akin to seductions.

"Reduce the weight of the pound
Or an ounce? Wait, better yet!
Let's help all writers and learners,
Reduce the length of our alphabet!"

"In a savings of paper and of time,
Let us do a consonant whittle:
Take an extraneous letter,
Right smack out of the middle."

So counting on fingers,
And mouthing each letter,
They selected the "N."
Just what could be better?

Then they broadcast to all
With a slight condescend,
"We have finally ended the
Continued use of the 'N.'"

Then heard on the streets,
In much that was written
The results of the alphabet's
Fate, so badly smitten.

Once we would have said:
"He went round the bend."
Now comes out, sadly:
"He wet roud the bed!"

Shadows on the Clouds

When spring winds change
And change yet again,
To new ways,
The rising sun shows
The direction of east,
The dark delays.

Piling weather fronts
Build like shrouds,
That's when you see
Shadows on the clouds.

Careful

You've just sustained

A hurtful slight,
And now you're boiling
For a fight.

You grab a can of
Pepper Spray
To gain the edge
In the fray.

But while your nose
Is still disjointed,
Remember where
The nozzle's pointed!

Wait 'til Sunday

"Mom," I asked, between my sobs,
"What's going to happen to me?"
"You will be healed and feeling fine.
Wait until Sunday, you will see."

These words she said between
Her own tears held, tight and close.
"The doctors have done their best.
And promise just one more dose."

Then head down, eyes shut tight,
She touched my chin her special way.
"I'm feeling the truth and right,
You are better! It feels like Sunday."

She was right. I heard the bells.

You Are Missed

It seems the weight
Of weeks past,
Life's colors fade.
Softer sunsets
With no afterglow.
Nights moving
With Shaded Stars.
Morning's Promise,
muted.

Lonely is the feeling,
In muffled hours.

You are missed.

Limited Edition

His name was Angus Cradition,
Who held an enviable position.
He also would spout
To all those about:
"I am a Limited Edition."

Then years too late
He sought out a mate.
He long suffered and fought:
Looked where he ought not.

Finally met a stalwart named Gretta,
With hot lips like warmed-over chetta.
Each glance brought hot oil,
This love no one could spoil.
A vow they took for worse or betta.

Angus said,
"Only one condition:
For I'm a limited edition!
There will be no child
To drive us both wild.
That's my absolute position!"

Gretta said,
"I heard your only condition,
But I've got my own tradition.
I'll say this just once!
You're a miserable dunce,
You'll see me next in perdition!"

The Will of The Wind

A great wind rose up,
And knocked off my hat.
And when I hollered,
It smacked me down flat.

Then said I should see
More than I chose
And when I refused,
Grabbed at my nose.

I was lifted too high
Into rarified sky,
Then sat on a
Soft cloud, with care.

"Let me now show you"
I heard the great wind,
scared me just silly,
'Til I felt I did sin!

It tipped over a mountain
Sent it into the sea,
Caused such a great splash,
A large fish kissed my knee!

From then 'til December
I've tried to remember
What happened, when.
But I can't!

Sidney the Cat

I was all alone that afternoon,
Just chatting with the cat.
Asking him how he was,
With thoughts of this and that.
He gave me a look that said:
"I'll say nothing," in nothing flat.

I saw his hair was matted,
And how he was a trouble.
He glared, wide eyed,
I swore he was seeing double.

We went on like that, my voice,
Obviously not compelling.
For the many questions asked,
He simply wasn't telling.

It was then we both decided
To go our separate ways.
He gave his high tail wave.
He wouldn't speak for days.

But that's the way we are.
Me and Sidney the cat.
I speak—he gives me a look,
says nothing, in nothing flat.

The Grin Reader

There he sits, straight as an arrow,
Eyes locked, smiling out his charm.
The floor director starts him up
With a simple dropping of an arm.

Firmly he reads the rolling prompter
Of mayhem, murder, and genocide,
Through the forest fires and killing quakes
His smile seems to grow, twice as wide.

He says it all with up-fixed brows;
Of crashing cars and broken laws.
Then sports, comments, and wild rumors
Enunciated through smile trembling jaws.

He repeats the darkest and fiercest news,
Still speaking in a warm and even meter
Of cheating and lying in our government
He has now morphed into the grin reader.

Just Relax!

We've been told with chide and scold,
To let it go, let it be, forget the gold.

Sit down and wait for the pressure to drop,
Think something else, "A full belly flop?"

Believe that when life goes frenetic.
It's not your parents, it's not genetic.

You've too much to do, letters to write,
Or e-mail. I've got that just about right?

Your eyes have a tick, your fingers drum.
Caught in an odd song, you mentally hum.

Time to forget jobs constructed in stacks,
To lean back, stomp out, and tip over racks.

Gain a posture of slumped resignation,
And be branded as full degeneration.

There are no programs, thirty-day cures,
No slogans, no path to get what is yours,

Now the hardest task you've ever tried,
And you feel you've cheated, maybe lied?

Next unwanted, marked as unreliable
You miss the attention, it's not deniable.
Leave now, find a space under a tree.
Think of nothing in all that you see.
Insist it is too far to walk, too far to talk.

Sail off in a mentally cool, evening sea,
Begin to breathe life as it's meant to be!

A Hundred Shades of Gold

A view from any window demands
You cast your eyes on the grove;
Witness the sight of sudden wealth
It's nature's giving treasure trove.

You cannot see beyond this sight
Overwhelming color yet unspoiled,
Untouched by wind or heavy rain
Each huge tree is crowned in gold.

The world awaits the changes coming
Even in a quiet day, unheard sighing
Knowing a season so soon gone;
Majestic view announcing dying.

Far too quickly comes a change:
raging winds and slanting rain.

Driving now lustrous gold
To lying soft on hungry ground.
Confirm the cycle of renewal
Revive with certainty rebound.

Now in this gifted moment,
A time to laugh and to hold
Witness as wondrous vision:
A hundred shades of gold.

Watch That Eagle

He can strike blazing fast
That's for the dog
So, put away the chickens
And all cats and calves,
Keep your eyes wide open!
But for your job
You be mopin'.

Winter Solace

Shake out the folds
Of the flannel
In your mind.

Make a cozy
Tent of them

To sit beneath,
Warm,
Comfortable.

And enjoy the quiet
Grace of winter.

Making Pathways for Chipmunks

Is just plain fun
See them scurry past quickest,
Always on the run.

There needs to be a place
That is a closed abide
Where with tail held high,
They can run and hide.

They do like bird food
And dried corn
You will likely find
The bag is torn.

Making pathways for chipmunks
You will see,
Is just as fun
As it can be!

If You Go into The Woods Today

Grab your gear and start the jeep,
Alert the one with whom you sleep.
It's time to camp in peace and quiet
And offer blood to mosquito's diet.

Think first of the ones, deer or wood
The type that are sadly called a tick.
That burrow deep into the skin,
And settle to munch, firmly stick.

There are some that cause deep pain,
Tiny, small as a beach sand grain.
The others larger, easier to spot.
They still itch and scare a lot.

Some large flyers, just as harsh
Found near the marsh.
These hurt to make you cry.
Called a horse, or deer fly.

Still you shrug, park, and pitch the tent.
Start a fire, open a Bud, become content.
The food goes way up high,
fooling a hungry bear.
If one attacks,
it's something rare.

Soon, all is quiet. you snuggle in
Just before the wind and rain begin.
Listen to the tent flaps, flap, flap,
Water hurries your sleep, to a snap.

Small currents seep beneath the bedding,
With no note of where it's heading.
For warmth, you together snuggle.
And coin the phrase, "Puddle Cuddle."

When You Get Back

Are words you heard
In early years:
To school
To work
To war
First spoken through a Mother's tear:
"When you get back, I'll be here."

In mid-life you too, have said:
To child
To teen
To young adult
Still spoken through a Mother's tear:
"When you get back, I'll be here."

Then later in your life, you have repose
To dream
To love
To believe
These same words said through the tears,
Were spoken too, and through us all:
God passed, given, blessed; a call:
To remember well and in good cheer:
"When you get back, I'll be here."

Our 1930s Home

"Come on in, we're always home."
Are words we usually said.
"There's a pot warming on the stove,
And one more beneath the bed."

Come on in and grab a chair,
This house is such a mess.
Let's trade a brand-new rumor.
Yep, the coffee's mostly fresh.

Please don't mind the kerosene lamp.
It's nearly full, the wick's been set.
I need to clean the smoky chimney.
First, let's share the coffee, I'll get.

There's plenty of new catalogs
In the outhouse, just out back.
Skip from using the shiny pages,
Mixed up in the paper stack.

We've heard nails a popping,
On a true hard freezing night.
But now the stove is firing hot.
I'll jar the door, just a mite.

'Cause the stove's so hot,
I'll toss on a sprig of pine.
It'll curl and quickly burn
The air will be, simply fine.

Come spring we'll get the electrical,
Maybe later, we'll add a phone.
For now, we get along quite fine.
Do come often; we're always home.

Create the Day

Let the day come slowly
The sun hides the dark.
Soft fog settles as dew
Harvest dreams, embark.

Let the day pace slowly,
Slip to middle morning.
Listen, apply a promise,
Apply the noon's horning.

Annual Visit

The doctor told me:
"Listen to your body!"
But my body knows
I eat for a hobby.

Neat stuff, Peanut Butter
New apples? Never!
Herring, Ice Cream,
Fried Chicken Liver.

TV commercials have me
Worried, really, really, bad.
With folks touting drugs
For what I've never had.

It's side effects I fear,
Make you stutter, go blind.
Have uncatchable breath,
With itch, bowels that bind.

Then they
Top off the list
Of diseases I've missed;
Ones titled as horrible,
But magically curable.

Another Day Off

I just took a day off
From taking a day off.

You ask, "What can this mean?"
It is nothing you have ever seen!

It is as if you are
Vacantly staring down a hole
Just sitting, gazing, like
Watching church bells toll.

A time when you can
Hear an angel's aching cry,
And feel her cotton soft
Breath caught in a timid sigh.

Then a day off taken from
A day off does truly allow
Each one of use, to be both
In the "then" and the "now."

Inactive, quiet, thinking nothing
Lets the days off be relevant,
Learning secrets, capturing truth
In knowing where the river went.

A flicker like a quickened spider web
Lets the cooling water begin its freeze;
Lying there, feeling ghostly brushes,
On welcoming skin, a warming breeze.

Easily snatching up the frothing seventh
Wave, as it gathers a final cresting.
And with strength filled mind, swing it
Wildly overhead to the ocean's resting.

Marrisa

There was once a small girl
I knew,
Who had a smile that grew
And grew.
A while went by, as it passed,
We were aghast.
The smile had fully spread
All round her pretty head.
A smile that started
Just for fun,
Did now completely,
Hide the sun.
Anytime our thoughts are
Dark as night
And we all want to see
Things go bright,
We remember the little
Girl I knew
Who had a smile that
Grew and grew.

Admit It! You Are Wrong!

I don't know if you really care,
You've made a grievous error.

You know the route you've taken,
Only verifies you're mistaken.

Even if you think you're right,
Chew it over through the night!

You can argue, have your say,
I will note: "You've gone astray."

Beyond your choice of woeful song,
Admit it, you are just plain wrong!

Seasons

The promise begins in the March side of the year,
With straining buds that herald much good cheer.

Then through treetops come the softest sigh,
To alert the forest that cleansing rains are nigh.

On cue, the aspen gently flutters its veil of leaves,
Happily announcing the arrival of a warming breeze.

Unrecorded time is passing through it all,
While night birds are practicing their call.

At last we revel in the truly fruitful month,
The promised stage.
As July, reveals nature's most bountiful,
And wondrous rage.

A Place In My Mind For You

There is a place in my mind
For wild comments is the why,
Ideas piled high as the sky,
Memories, wild near to fly.
Here's what friends may say
Come into my mind and stay.

Night Walk

A quiet night for walking,
A new moon,
Bearded by gliding clouds.
A quiet night for walking,
Night birds crying
In mystic pain.
A quiet night for walking,
Rocks tickle water,
Sweeping around.
A quiet night for walking
Angels moving,
Light, free,
Dancing on moonbeams.
A quiet night for walking,
Calling up more memories,
Afraid to forget,
A quiet night for walking,
Cleansing worn dreams.

Election Time Lament

When we can't afford tomorrow

And can't budget enough for today.

We've not gone beyond our means,

But forced to cancel most of dreams.

By salary cuts and layoff schemes,

Final salary sums aggrieve our sorrow

And prove we can't afford tomorrow.

Rivershore Books

www.rivershorebooks.com
info@rivershorebooks.com
www.facebook.com/rivershore.books
www.twitter.com/rivershorebooks

www.ingramcontent.com/pod-product-compliance
Lightning Source LLC
LaVergne TN
LVHW051603080426
835510LV00020B/3104